A PRESSED FLOWER KEEPSAKE BOOK

Text and Illustrations by
Louise Kollenbaum

Souvenirs de Fleurs

CHRONICLE BOOKS

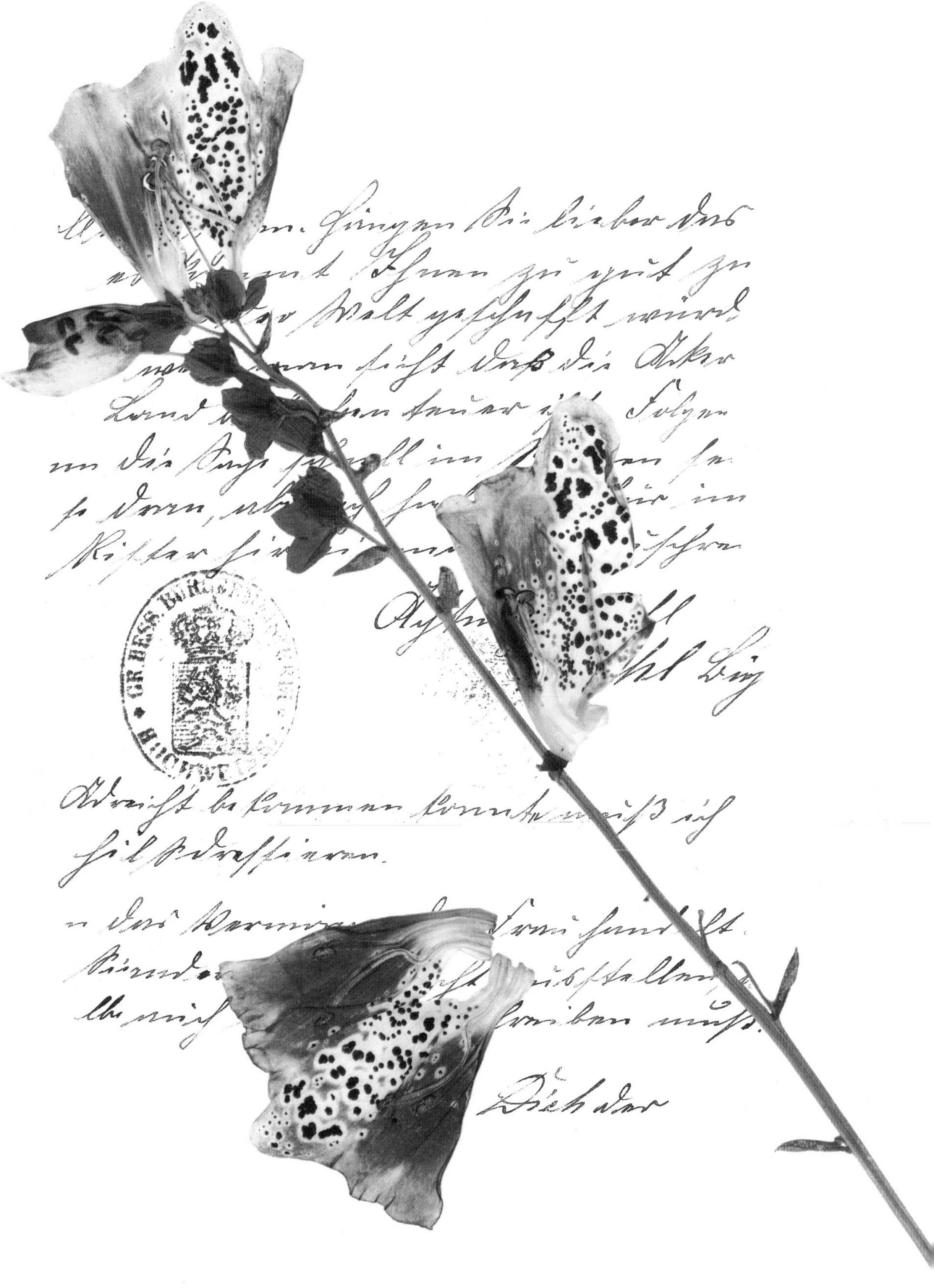

F o r   A m y

In memory of my father, John C. Kollenbaum
who first brought me into the garden.

PERMISSIONS:

Gertrude Jekyll:
Children and Gardens. Reproduced by permission of the Antique Collectors' Club, New York.

Vita Sackville-West:
Passenger to Tehran copyright © 1926 Vita Sackville-West

Vita Sackville-West's Garden Book copyright © The Estate of Vita Sackville-West. Reproduced by permission of Curtis Brown, London.

Text and illustrations: Louise Kollenbaum
Title Calligraphy: Elvis Swift

10 9 8 7 6 5 4 3 2 1

ISBN: 0-8118-1956-6

Printed in Hong Kong

Distributed in Canada by
Raincoast Books
8680 Cambie Street
Vancouver, B.C. V6P 6M9

CHRONICLE BOOKS

85 Second Street
San Francisco, CA 94105
www.chronbooks.com

Design: Miranda Design, San Francisco

Although pressing flowers is a solitary pursuit, *Souvenirs de Fleurs* is a collaboration. I would like to thank the gifted Charles Mize for his talent and his perseverance. I could not have created the images without him.

Charlotte Kollenbaum and Gwen Pettus pressed along with me. I am grateful for their knowledge and support.

Thanks also to Sharon Silva for her thoughtful help with the text and her unflagging sense of humor, Debra Ginsberg for her valuable contributions, Renate Stendahl and Kim Chernin for their insights, Bruni and Edgar Neumann for their translations, Janis Donnaud and Charlotte Sheedy for their advice and friendship, David Wiegand for his musical inspiration, Orlan at World Litho for his help, Park for her generosity and spirit, Caroline Herter and Debra Lande of Chronicle Books, and Liz Miranda of Miranda Design for their faith in the project.

This book is dedicated to Amy Rennert with gratitude for the inexpressible.

INTRODUCTION

The idea for Souvenirs de Fleurs was inspired by a day in the country. I was vacationing with friends in California's Napa Valley. We were staying at a winery in a rambling old stone house overlooking the vineyard. The property was grand, slightly run-down, and very romantic. Ghostlike impressions were imbedded in the stone where once crawling vines had been. A few dangling branches hung from well-worn trellises. The grounds suggested a past era. The garden was well-tended and bountiful with flowers and vegetables. We spent the day lazing about—reading, sketching, and writing, interspersed with short walks shaded by olive trees.

The next morning, my friends set out for the market while I stayed behind to pick some flowers from the garden to press. I began gathering late enough to avoid any dew that might remain from the night before. I had asked the permission of the winery owners to pick, so only the bees seemed to mind as I gathered many flowers I didn't recognize.

With a bundle in hand, I returned to the house and cleared a work area. The door was open, and in the background I could hear the faint, tinny sound of a small portable radio tuned to a Tex-Mex station. The air was sweet and festive. My friends soon returned with bags of food. It was our vacation ritual to put together elaborate brunches, with each person choosing something special—freshly baked bread, sweet butter, a round of creamy chevre, a wedge of well-veined Gorgonzola, a small bowl of herb-packed Nicoise olives. We usually ended with something very chocolate and very rich.

I worked in the living room as my friends prepared our feast in the adjoining kitchen. I could hear them laughing and talking as I began to separate the flowers for pressing. I stripped away the unnecessary leaves, removed unwanted dirt and bugs, and eliminated a petal or flower here and there. I looked closely, in awe of the variety of color and the complexity of the botanical structure found inside a single plant. All the while, I tried to imagine what the flowers would look like once pressed. Soon, my small field press was filled up. With what was left, I put together a small arrangement for our table.

As I worked that day, I wrote down my thoughts and drew small sketches on various scraps of paper—modest records that have kept that experience vivid in my memory to this day. It was then that I decided to design a special book in which I could keep pressed flowers and my reminiscences in a single place. Within this journal you will find simple guides to gathering, pressing, storing, and mounting flowers; a brief history of Victorian flower pressing and florigraphy; blank pages on which to sketch or write; newsprint pages for temporary pressing; and translucent sleeves for storing and easy viewing of your flowers once they are fully pressed—the perfect place to record special days, warm memories, and fleeting thoughts. Now, it's your turn.

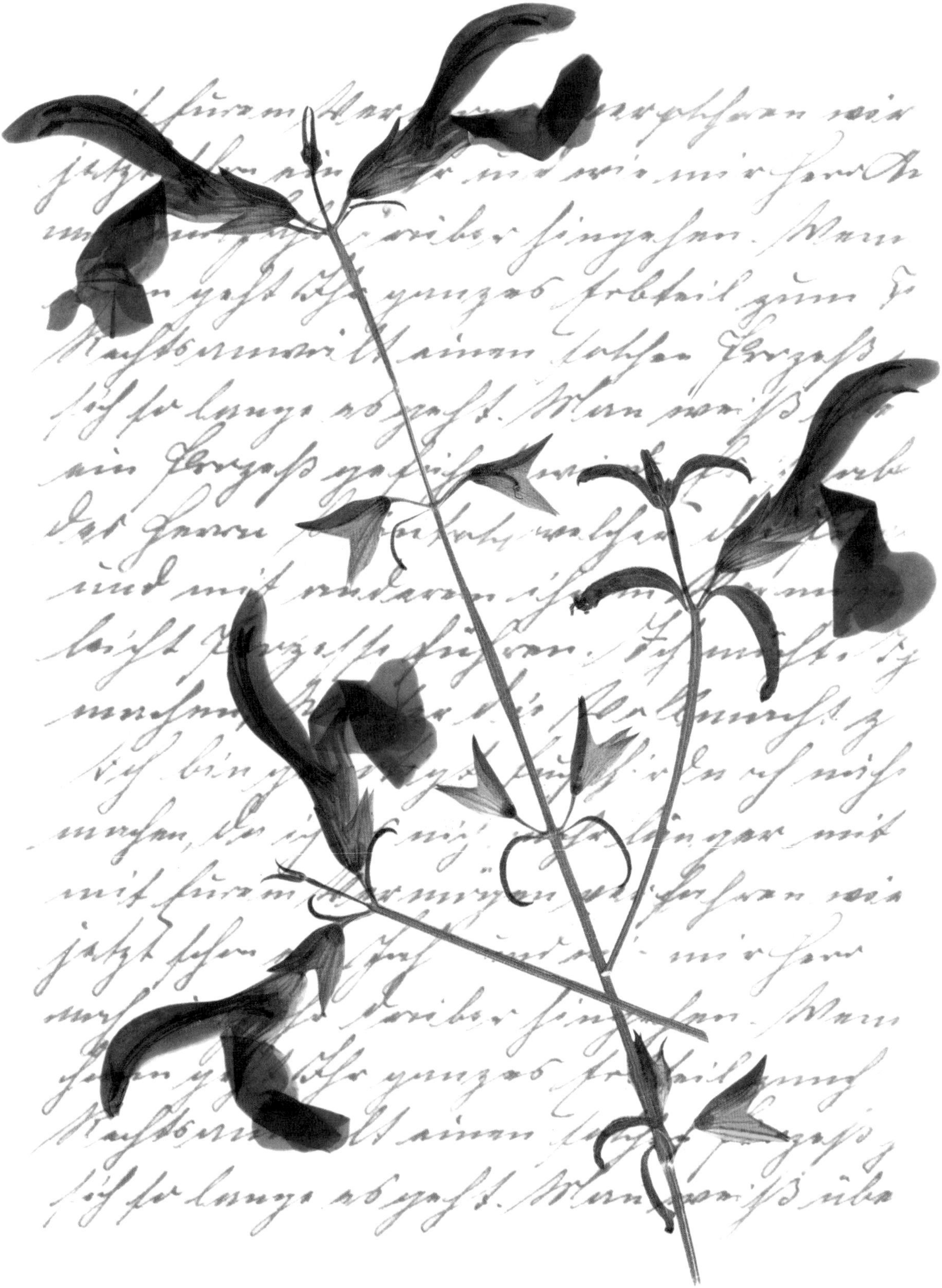

WHAT YOU NEED TO GET STARTED

The only equipment you need for pressing flowers is the press itself.
I started with a small field press—just large enough to hold a few flowers, some extra petals, and a portion of the stem on a page. I was immediately fascinated, and when friends learned I was pressing, they began giving me a variety of presses as gifts.

I received a press from France with Giverny written on the top, a marketing reference to Monet's inspired garden (although no one is allowed to pick there). It was only about three inches square, but I took it everywhere and started filling it immediately. Weeks later I discovered that the paper layer, which holds the flowers between sheets of blotter paper and corrugated cardboard, had a textured surface. The paper's pattern had transferred onto the petals. So, if you decide to buy an assembled press, don't be seduced by attractive packaging alone.

Flower Presses

Flower presses come in all sizes and prices, but most are composed of essentially the same elements: newsprint, blotter paper, and corrugated cardboard in a wooden frame fastened with straps or screws for adjusting pressure. For a temporary press (until you can put your flowers into a heavier permanent press), you can use the newsprint pages provided at the back of this journal.

Most professional botanists use a twelve-by-eighteen-inch press made up of a pair of two-inch-lattice wood frames bound by two buckled straps. The lattice design allows for more efficient drying, and the straps may be loosened to accommodate more flowers or tightened for additional pressure as plant materials shrink. Newsprint for pressing and later transferring the flowers, heavy blotter paper (roughly hundred pound) for absorbing any excess moisture, and corrugated cardboard, which has an inner fluted layer that allows for good air circulation, come packed in the press. I use this type of press because of its large format. I can press more flowers and larger ones.

Smaller, lighter presses are available in many craft stores and herbarium supply stores. They generally have the same components as the professional press, although newsprint is not always included. These lightweight presses are good for carrying along when you're gathering in the fields.

You can make your own press with two rectangular pieces of plywood and four bolts, wing nuts, and washers, fastening one set at each corner. You will need to purchase the newsprint, blotter paper, and cardboard separately. Tightening or loosening the wing nuts adjusts the pressure. You can also use nylon webbing straps instead of the bolts for fastening the plywood frames.

If you want to start more simply, begin with the classic tool for pressing flowers: a metropolitan telephone directory. This is a heavy book, with lots of room to place the flowers between several layers of absorbent pages. If you use this method, be sure to place extra weight, such as several bricks, on top. Telephone directories are also great for storing already-pressed flowers.

In addition to this journal and permanent press, you will need the following items to begin your pressed-flower collection.

Other Tools and Materials

◆ Scissors for cutting flowers and various materials.

◆ Newsprint for pressing, if not included with press.

◆ Paper clips, unfolded and round edged, for easing pressed flowers off paper.

◆ Tweezers (rounded tip) for handling delicate pressed flowers.

◆ Exacto knife for trimming pressing flowers.

◆ White glue, if mounting your pressed flowers.

HOW TO GATHER FLOWERS FOR PRESSING

My friend Mary is an avid wildflower explorer. One early spring, we drove to Chimney Rock in Point Reyes, California, a location well known for its fertile ground during March and April. Initially, this was an exercise in restraint for me, since hikers are not allowed to pick the flowers that grow on this government land. But then something wonderful happened. I spent the day "window shopping" for what I might eventually gather elsewhere and press. The fields were not yet in full bloom. At a glance, just a few spots of color were visible. Yet looking more closely, I discovered pussy ears, mallow, and a magnificent bluish purple Douglas iris. Even just preparing for gathering can be an exercise in concentration and revelation.

Gathering is the first step in the pressing process. Remember to use this journal to note thoughts and details and to draw simple sketches to help you recapture the moment later.

There are a few basic points to keep in mind as
you gather your flowers for pressing.

- Always choose flowers that are in the best condition possible. Try to select specimens that appear healthy, remembering that their color is richest early in the budding process. Shake or blow your flowers gently to remove any insects that may be hiding in the petals.

- Since moisture of any kind causes flowers to mildew or turn brown or black when pressed, try to gather your flowers as close to noon as possible. This will avoid morning or evening dew. If you find any moisture on the flower, shake the blossom gently to remove the dampness. As the light of day fades, flowers begin to close up. What you pick will be exactly what you press, another reason to select your flowers in the middle of the day when the petals are open and dry.

- Try to gather flowers of a similar thickness for the same pressing. If there are several flowers on the same page, the thicker flowers will prevent the thinner ones from drying properly.

- The best time to press flowers is immediately upon picking them. Flowers wilt or discolor quickly, especially wildflowers, so it is always a good idea to have a portable press handy. If you are not traveling with a press, use the newsprint pages in the back of this journal for temporary storage, or place the flowers between the pages of a book. Another option is to bring along an airtight plastic bag. Place the flowers in the bag, then blow in air and seal tightly. I haven't had any success with this method, however, so I try always to tote my portable press.

- As you gather, it is important to keep in mind that most flowers require some form of preparation before they can be pressed. Some flowers, such as a thick rose, will not dry properly unless dismantled–the petals separated and the stem removed–otherwise, mildew and discoloration will result. The daffodil is another example. It must be sliced in half and the front leaves removed so that no overlapping occurs when pressed. A pansy, on the other hand, requires no preparation because of its simple petal structure; it can be clipped and pressed as is.

- Experimentation is the key to success with pressing. I recommend gathering simple flowers like Iceland poppies to start and then moving on to the more complex.

♦ Some flowers are poisonous or rare and thus protected by law, so be mindful when gathering. Always attempt to secure permission before picking flowers on private or government property.

Choosing and picking the flowers you will eventually press is an exciting first step. Try describing the flower in this journal, noting down its shape, color, and texture, along with the date and time you picked it, for a permanent record of your finds. As you press more, you develop particular favorites. If you find that these are difficult to locate again, or if you are not allowed to pick them, consider starting your own garden for pressing.

THE ART OF PRESSING FLOWERS

The art of pressing flowers is a journey in experimentation, patience, and acceptance. When I began, I was intimidated. I pressed only the flowering portion of the plant, and selected only a few kinds of flowers. As I got further into the process, my eye began to wander, and I started seeing the flower's construction—the intricacies of the stems and leaves. I began to press as much of the flower as would fit on the page, appreciating it in its entirety. Now I'm eager to press as many different flowers as possible.

Respect the process. Modern day anxiety demands that we get things done fast, but flower pressing is made up of deliberate stages of experience, each intelligently informing the next. If your first pressed flowers don't turn out the way you anticipated, try to enjoy what they look like anyway and move on to your next press. With luck, many of them will form beautiful compositions naturally and retain much of their original color. Even so, be prepared for some to turn brown or for leaves to fold over awkwardly onto themselves.

Press many different flowers. You may find that in the beginning your success rate is low, but you'll likely also discover that every flower, once saved, has its own beauty. There is no single correct way to press. The methods for pressing vary as much as the people who press.

There are a few constants to keep in mind as you go about developing your own personal style.

♦ Clean off an area large enough for your press and flowers.

♦ Choose a time when you won't be interrupted and set a mood. Wagner played at high volume is just the audio inspiration I need.

♦ Place a piece of corrugated cardboard from your press on a flat surface, then place a piece of blotter paper on top of the cardboard. Next, fold a sheet of newsprint in half—your flowers will be stored between the two layers. Place a second piece of blotter paper on top, and then a second piece of cardboard. This same "sandwich" will be used for every pressing.

♦ Spread out your flowers and edit your selection according to variety and thickness.

♦ Choose a flower to press and look at it carefully. Keep in mind that what you press between the pages is going to be exactly what appears in the final product. Therefore, unless that little bug is part of your overall aesthetic, remove it now. Remember, too, that you are seeing the flower in three dimensions at this point. Try to imagine what it will look like once it is flattened.

♦ When you are ready to put the flower down, remember to place it between the newsprint layers. Using your fingers or tweezers, experiment with designs, pressing one leaf over the other, or placing one petal atop another. When dealing with translucent petals, this overlapping effect will intensify a fragile color, but with the more opaque petals, overlapping will darken and cloud the effect.

♦ If you are pressing more flowers, repeat the process, assembling additional "sandwiches" atop the first one and making the stack only as high as will fit in the press. Place the stack in your press and tighten the pressure. Place the press in a well-ventilated, dry spot.

♦ Good and consistent pressings take six to eight weeks. Avoid peeking during the pressing period. I know it's difficult, but it is worth the wait.

♦ To recognize if a flower is fully dried, hold it upright by its stem. Using a pair of tweezers, lift it off the newsprint. The rounded tip of an unfolded paper clip works beautifully to loosen any petals that are stuck to the page. If the flower

stands without bending, it is dry. Now slip the flower into one of the sleeves provided in this journal.

◆ Once pressed, the flowers should never be placed in direct sunlight. They are very fragile at this stage and must be handled with care.

Flowers fade when they are pressed. I love to watch the changing colors, enjoying each one in turn. I have learned to appreciate the look of faded flowers. Sometimes the final result delights me more than the color of the flower in full bloom.

SUGGESTIONS FOR PRESSING

Let common sense be your guide as you begin gathering flowers for pressing. I learned early on to expect and appreciate any outcome from my efforts. If you want to increase your success rate, avoid very thick flowers such as ranunculuses and marigolds, those with a high water content and waxy leaves such as succulents, and flowers that grow in a dense cluster, or inflorescence, like hydrangea and allium. The following list, while not foolproof, should prove helpful. It comes from my own experience and suggestions from experts.

Keep in mind that some of these flowers, such as salvia and nepeta, come in many forms, and that not all of them will press easily. I hope that you will not limit yourself to what is listed here, that you will press any flower that interests you.

ALYSSUM PANSY

BUTTERCUP

BLUEBELL

COMMON FOXGLOVE

ANEMONE

CLEMATIS

DELPHINIUM MALLOW

NEPETA

COLUMBINE

LOVE-IN-A-MIST

SNOWDROP

CROCUS

FORGET-ME-NOT

SALVIA

GRAPE HYACINTH

PRIMROSE

DAISY GOLDENROD

LOBELIA

PRIMULA VIOLA

FUCHSIA

LARKSPUR

ICELAND POPPY

JOHNNY-JUMP-UP

GERANIUM

LISIANTHUS

Create your own list from your successes and failures using this journal for creative documentation on what works and why.

Tuesday 29" 1851

Wensday 9 / Peleg G Thurston Dr
// To hove to Moove Ayurtus
// to cash 25

3 / Elisha Pyne & Co Dr
// hove david Mathewra
// to cash 2 00

9 9 / Marvin Smith Dr
// hove to citty .... „ 62

Thursday / Steven Phillips R 2
Friday / cash .... „

107 / Christopher Hudric Dr
// Load To cloth 160
// To 6 B cotton citty

Friday / Olney Henric Dr
aug 8 / To 1 Load cotton 6 Bales 3358 lb
107 / 1 boat .... molaco

/ Christopher Duffee Dr
// To hove & wagon 2 to citty 50
// to finish 2

/ Daniel Peck Dr
5 / To hove & chane 2 days .... R 2

/ Wm H King Dr

HOW TO STORE YOUR
OVERFLOW OF PRESSED FLOWERS

*Like many artists, I am a collector by nature. My pressed-flower col-*lection exists mostly for the few exquisite moments of discovery I enjoy when I take it out

for an occasional viewing. I find it difficult to accept the temporal nature of pressed

flowers—they fade with age. Viewing the flowers, exposing them to the elements, and try-

ing out different arrangements means they will age even more quickly. Since my primary

goal is to preserve the collection, I handle my pressed flowers only rarely.

There are two good storage methods for keeping your overflow of pressed flowers once

you have slipped your current favorites into the sleeves of this journal. The first is to use

old metropolitan telephone directories, as they are heavy enough to keep the flowers flat.

Use different books for flowers of different sizes. Within each book, you might order

them according to their season of bloom, their color, or their size. Also, remember to check after you've removed a specimen to make sure that the remaining contents have not shifted. If too many flowers gather toward the spine, they may break when you close the book.

Transparent envelopes, the type used by coin and stamp collectors, are also good for storage. They allow you to determine the contents at a glance. Label the envelopes with all relevant information for easy checking of what you have and may want to use, and then store them in a closed sturdy box or other container. Or you may store them in a box between the folds of newsprint, piling the sheets flat and adding a piece of corrugated cardboard to the stack every now and again for good ventilation.

Keep in mind the following tips when storing pressed flowers.

◆ Always work with great care when handling the flowers, for they are delicate and brittle. I recommend using tweezers to transfer them from the press into storage.

◆ Store the flowers where air circulation is good. Avoid damp areas, as mildew is a serious threat.

◆ Do not expose the flowers to direct sunlight, and strive to keep the temperature constant.

No matter what method you use for storage, remember to organize and label your material for easy access. Flowers you choose to store today might be transferred to this journal or used for creative projects in the future.

Chapter Six

HOW TO MOUNT PRESSED FLOWERS

If you're planning to use your pressed flowers instead of storing them, you will need to mount them on some type of surface. The flowers will be delicate at this stage, and they can break easily. The rounded edge of an unfolded paper clip helps nudge stubborn petals from the newsprint or blotter paper. It's important to decide on your designs before you begin the actual mounting, as it's almost impossible to move the flowers after they have been secured in place.

Here are some ideas on how to mount pressed flowers, including tips to ensure their longevity.

◆ Whenever possible, use 100 percent acid-free paper. The absence of chemicals helps the pressed flowers last longer.

◆ I use ordinary white glue because it's easy. Professionals often use herbarium glue because it doesn't become brittle over time and some kinds enable you to remove the specimen. (For more information about the different mounting materials available, contact an herbarium supply company.) Use a toothpick to dot the strongest part of the flower (usually the stem, if attached) with the glue. Too much glue will show through the flowers, so apply it sparingly in a very thin layer. Also, most glues have a sheen in certain light, so avoid getting any on your mounting surface.

◆ Another popular mounting method is to use clear contact paper with adhesive on one side. Trapping the flower between the contact paper and the mounting surface can be a little tricky, however. The best way to do this is to roll back the backing sheet from the contact paper and arrange the flower on the backing. Then, roll the contact paper back over the backing—the flower will adhere to it. You are now ready to place the contact paper (with flower attached) onto your mounting surface. The contact paper method is a good one for creating projects such as bookmarks, which require some sturdiness and protection for the flowers.

◆ Herbarium specimens are sometimes attached with a special thin linen tape. To use the tape, place small strips of it on strategic parts of the stem to secure the flower to the mounting surface.

◆ If you are framing a design, make sure that the frame is airtight to prevent any air or dampness from reaching the flower.

◆ Avoid displaying mounted flowers in direct sunlight. Even if they are framed and protected by glass, they will eventually fade. Place them in indirect light only.

107

Oney Hewitt Dr

1 Load To _____ 93 ℔ Cloth 160

Friday ___ To _____ cotton _____ Dr

To _____ _____ 3358 ℔

1 _____ _____ Sunday

Christopher Dutee Dr

To hoe & wagon 2 to city 75¢   1.50
       "   to Muthill   25

_____ Peck Dr

& chaise 2 days — 3.00

_____ _____ Dr

_____ labour _____   .50

_____ J Barnes Dr
                    wife mothers
To hire & toped Buggee to his

Peleg G Thurst_____
    To cash on acct

Elisha Eyre Dr
To more to Natic with _____
Mother _____ verbal order   1.50

Wm Thurstin Dr

CREATIVE IDEAS FOR PRESSED FLOWERS

There are countless possibilities for creative projects when working with pressed flowers. Before you begin on any of the ideas described here, you will want to give yourself enough space, turn on your favorite music, and allow for uninterrupted time so that you can experiment.

Think of your prep time as a warm-up. A musician tunes his or her instrument and plays the scales. An athlete stretches to loosen up muscles. As an artist, this is your time to anticipate and visualize.

Ask yourself some basic questions about composition. Is the look of your project clean and simple? Are you using one flower or several of the same kind of flower? Are the flowers all the same color? Or is your concept busy and boldly colorful, with flowers filling every corner? Consider the scale of the flowers next to one another. Is your composition centered and balanced or do you want something asymmetrical? Think about how the size and the color of a flower will influence your composition. Walk away often—a short break can provide a new perspective. Remember, nothing is permanent until mounted.

Stationery, Greeting Cards, Bookmarks

A pressed flower folded within a sheet of stationery is a charming and thoughtful idea—and it's easy. For greeting cards, use a small amount of glue to attach the flowers or simply tuck them loose into the fold. Vary the flowers you choose according to season or occasion, and add your own message or artwork to each design.

Invitations, bookmarks, and gift tags are easy to decorate because their small size requires only simple designs. For bookmarks, I recommend using a card stock and contact paper for mounting. The contact paper adds surface protection, while the card stock contributes durability. Mounting the flowers on white or lightly colored rice paper is also popular. Although the resulting bookmark is less resilient, the look is particularly lovely because of the paper's near translucence.

Herbaria

Consider assembling a personal herbarium, a collection arranged for clear and easy reference. Use a heavyweight acid-free paper for mounting, and space and glue the specimens according to your own pleasure. Label each plant according to its common name, Latin name, location, and use. Plan your herbarium as a series of separate pages or as a poster-sized arrangement framed and hung for display.

Framed Flowers

When her sister performed in a local play, my associate Debra asked for a few of the flowers from the opening night bouquet. She pressed some of the pansies and johnny-jump-ups, mounted a copy of the playbill on light-colored heavyweight paper, and then arranged the flowers loosely over it. She sealed the whole composition in a very simple all-glass picture frame. The result was a lasting memento from the performance. This idea works well for birthdays, weddings, anniversaries, and other special occasions.

Place Settings and Place Cards

Whenever I have company for dinner, I put a different pressed flower at each place setting, laying it on the plate or napkin. For formal dinners, my late friend David always took the time to mount a pressed flower on each guest's place card. I was so charmed that I always took mine home.

A BRIEF HISTORY OF PRESSING

An interest in pressing flowers and keeping records of plant specimens has flourished for centuries, but it was during the Victorian era that pressing reached its greatest popularity. Many Victorian women were able to spend their considerable leisure time strolling through their gardens or along country lanes, collecting and recording the blossoms they gathered. This pursuit had both romantic and scientific significance: pressed flowers given by admirers recalled a special moment, while catalogs of plants documented the specimens' evolution and uses. With their passion for sentiment and memorabilia, the Victorians turned flower pressing into an art form that continues to survive in today's fast-paced technological world.

Records of plant specimens can be found as far back as the fifteenth century, and it was from these first herbals that the Victorians took their lead. Early on, healers and physicians sought cures in herbs and flowers for numerous physical and mental complaints. Chamomile, for example, was taken to ease stomach ailments, and lavender was prescribed to quiet raging fevers.

As more local flora was used for medicine and the study of nature became more scientific, carefully cataloging each plant with its ascribed properties became necessary. The first herbaria, collections of pressed plants and flowers mounted and labeled as to location and use, were developed in the mid-sixteenth century to meet this need. The Victorians refined the concept, carefully documenting and classifying thousands of flowers and other plants. There are many herbaria in existence today, and studying them offers a valuable understanding of the plants and their history.

The Victorians were highly reserved but intensely sentimental. Influenced by their flower-loving Queen Victoria, women became interested in ornamental gardens, window boxes, and the use of flowers for making jewelry and cosmetics. An extensive knowledge of botany was considered to be an important part of a "lady's" education. She was expected to design and catalog the flowers in her own garden, as well as understand the healing and cosmetic properties of various herbs and plants. The intricate pressings that were the result showed off the extent of the presser's education and accomplishment.

The women of this era also viewed pressing flowers as a way to save their memories. In a time when flowers had their own symbolic language, specific blooms carried great meaning, especially those that had been the gift of a suitor. It was a diverting pastime, for example, to keep a diary of pressed flowers made up of bouquets received from friends and admirers. In the same spirit, letters or greeting cards bearing pressed flowers were sent in wintertime when fresh blooms were unattainable. The Flower Game, a common pastime for groups of Victorian women, was a way to foretell the future through pressed flowers. One or more flowers were glued to individual cards, and the cards were assembled into a deck. Each woman would blindly draw one card from the stack. The flower(s) mounted on the chosen card signified the traits of the player's future suitor.

The simple pleasure of saving a special flower remains unchanged from Victorian times. Flower pressing is still practiced for science, sentiment, and craft. People all over the country are pressing and then exhibiting their home-spun compositions in county fairs and sharing their knowledge in self-published newsletters.

The Victorians may have perfected the gentle art of flower pressing, but contemporary practitioners have kept it alive and flourishing.

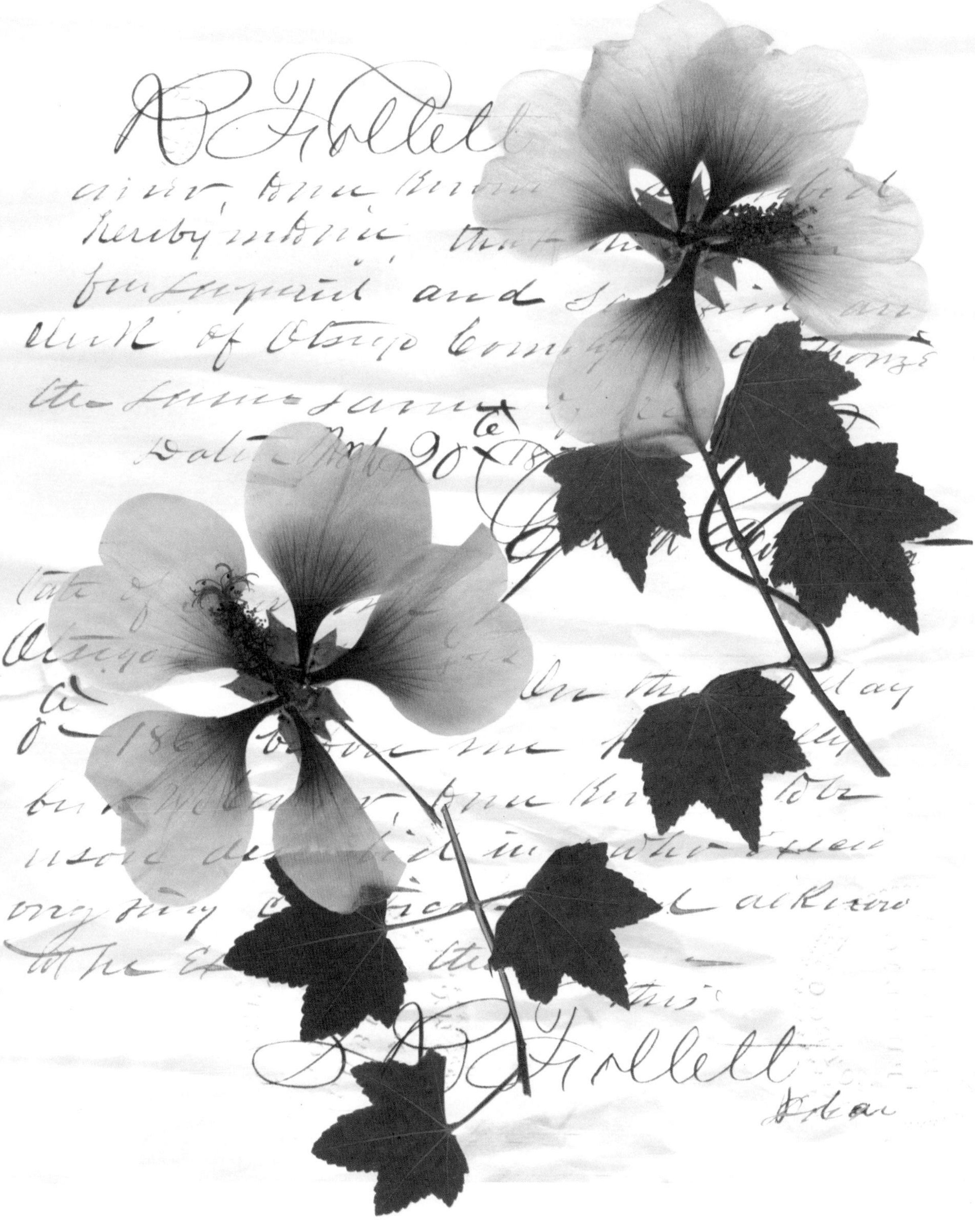

THE LANGUAGE OF FLOWERS

Although ascribing symbolic meanings to flowers dates back to ancient times, the notion of different flowers representing distinct feelings and ideas was reborn and flourished during the Victorian era. Just how this special "language," or florigraphy, found its way into nineteenth-century society is open to speculation, but at a time when open declarations of love were considered shocking, it is no surprise that the Victorians used the traditional symbolism of flowers (while adding some of their own) to communicate their emotions.

Greek mythology was the source for many flower meanings. Then, in medieval times, Europeans developed the Doctrine of Signatures. In part, the theory associated the physical characteristics of flowers or other plants with body parts they resembled. Walnut leaves, for example, came to be associated with wisdom, since a shelled walnut looks like the brain. The johnny-jump-up, shaped like the human heart, was assigned the meaning happiness, which was thought to originate in the heart.

Still another purported influence on Victorian flower meanings was Selam, a rhyming language of objects that was a popular means of unspoken communication in Turkish harems in the eighteenth century. Lady Mary Wortley Montagu, who was married to an English ambassador to Turkey, is credited with introducing this unique language to Britain in letters to friends, although there remains a question as to how much Selam actually contributed to Victorian floral symbolism.

The sentimental Victorians drew from all these sources to develop their language of flowers. By the mid-nineteenth century, dozens of dictionaries had been published that listed specific meanings for hundreds of flowers. Their appearance created some confusion, however, since the authors often created their own meanings as well as liberally plagiarized the dictionaries of others. In order to interpret correctly a poetic bouquet, or tussie-mussie, sent by a friend or admirer, it was essential that the two parties involved use the same dictionary. With literally hundreds of flowers and plants to choose from, people were able to carry on elaborate conversations without words, creating a pleasant and often highly romantic pastime. When fresh flowers were unavailable, gifts of pressed flowers, mounted and carefully arranged, formed the dialogues.

Today, with renewed interest in the healing properties of flowers and plants, florigraphy is experiencing a renaissance. Many of the traditional dictionaries remain in print (some of

the old ones with pressed flowers still folded into their pages) and new ones appear every couple of years. With a little knowledge of the ancient language of florigraphy and a sense of humor, your pressed flowers can take on new meanings.

Following is a list of some common flowers and their poetic connotations.

ACACIA: *friendship*

ALYSSUM: *worth beyond beauty*

ANEMONE: *expectation*

AZALEA: *first love*

BABY'S BREATH: *gentleness*

BACHELOR'S BUTTON: *hope in love*

BLUEBELL: *delicacy*

BUTTERCUP: *riches*

CALENDULA: *joy*

CALLA LILY: *feminine modesty*

CARNATION (RED): *passionate love*

CHAMOMILE: *energy in adversity*

DAFFODIL: *regard*

DAISY: *innocence*

DELPHINIUM: *heaven*

ELDERFLOWER: *compassion*

FORGET-ME-NOT: *true love*

FORSYTHIA: *good nature*

FREESIA: *innocence*

FUCHSIA: *confiding love*

GARDENIA: *secret love*

GERANIUM (ROSE): *preference*

GLADIOLUS: *strength of character*

GOLDENROD: *encouragement*

HEATHER: *beauty in solitude*

HONEYSUCKLE: *devoted affection*

HYDRANGEA: *boastfulness*

IRIS (BLUE): *message*

IVY: *wedded love*

JASMINE (WHITE): *amiability*

JOHNNY-JUMP-UP: *happiness*

LAVENDER: *luck*

LILAC (PURPLE): *first emotions of love*

LILY OF THE VALLEY: *return of happiness*

LOTUS FLOWER: *silence*

MAGNOLIA: *love of nature*

MARIGOLD: *sorrow*

NARCISSUS: *egotism*

NASTURTIUM: *patriotism*

NETTLE: *slander*

ORANGE BLOSSOM: *bridal festivities*

FLORIGRAPHY

PANSY: *tender thoughts*

PEONY: *bashfulness*

PRIMROSE (SCARLET): *pride*

QUEEN ANNE'S LACE: *protection*

RHODODENDRON: *danger*

ROSE (LAVENDER): *pure love*

ROSE (PINK): *grace*

ROSE (RED): *love*

ROSE (RED AND WHITE): *warmth of heart*

ROSE (YELLOW): *friendship*

ROSEMARY: *remembrance*

ST. JOHN'S WORT: *superstition*

SNAPDRAGON: *presumption*

SNOWDROP: *consolation*

SWEET PEA: *delicate pleasure*

THISTLE: *austerity*

TUBEROSE: *dangerous pleasure*

TULIP (PINK): *imagination*

TULIP (RED): *admiration*

TULIP (YELLOW): *hopeless love*

VIOLET (BLUE): *faithfulness*

VIOLET (WHITE): *modesty*

WALLFLOWER: *fidelity in misfortune*

WISTERIA: *welcome*

YARROW: *health*

ZINNIA: *thoughts of absent friends*

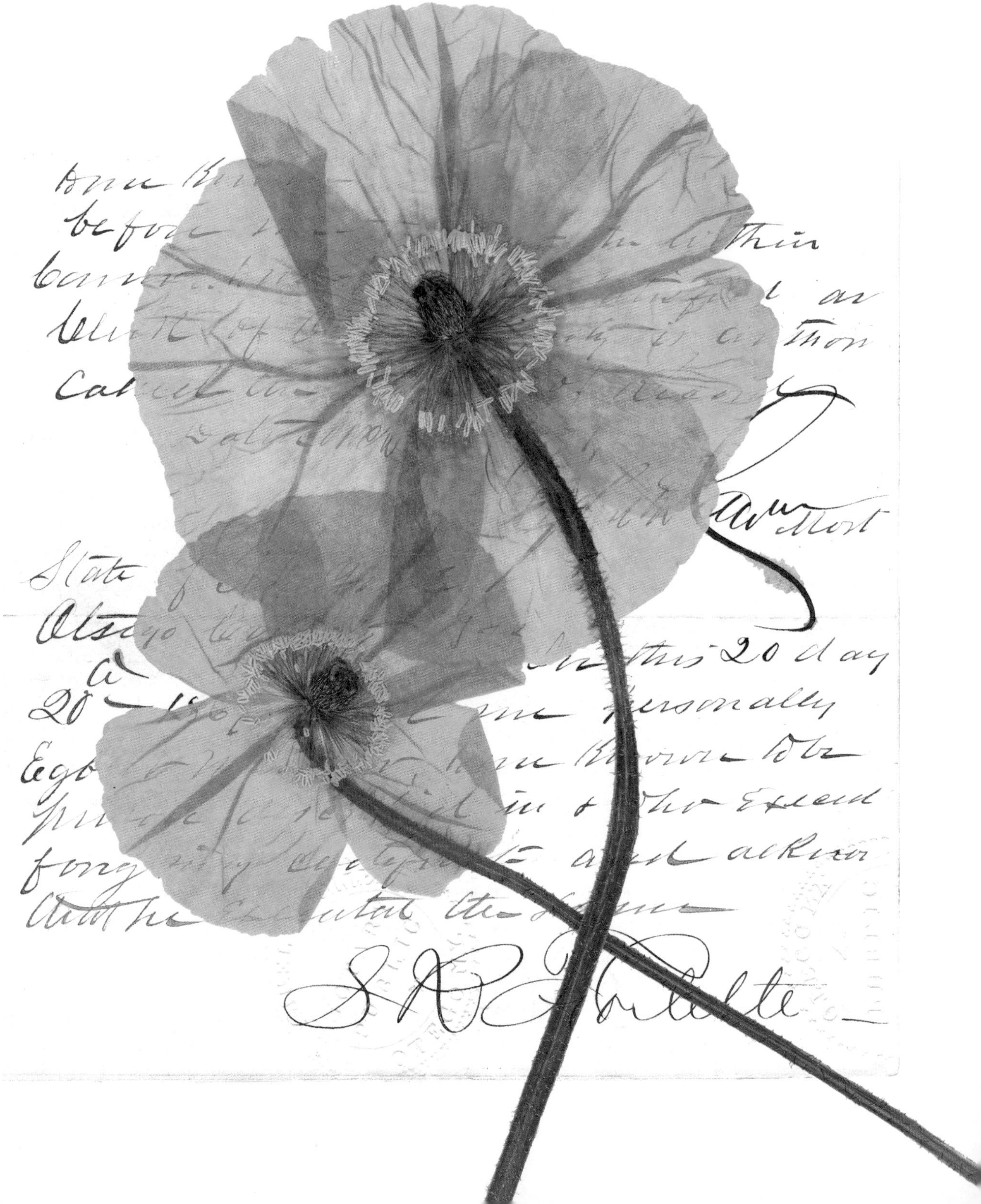
State
Otsego
this 20 day
personally

A SELECTIVE GLOSSARY

I'm not particularly good at recalling the names of people I meet. I'm more likely to remember some distinguishing characteristic. The same holds true for flowers and plants. Still, I feel it is only proper to make the effort.

My friend Park, a collector of all things imaginable, found the perfect birthday gift for me one year, *The First Book of Botany: Designed to Cultivate the Observing Powers of Children.* This simple learning guide, published in 1873, is filled with diagrams and brief descriptions. It provides me with just enough information to use the proper terms as I observe plants and flowers and as I begin to dismantle them.

What follows are some common botanical terms.

ANTHER: *the pollen-bearing part of the stamen*

ANTHESI: *the time of opening of a flower*

ANNUAL: *a plant that finishes its life cycle in a single growing season*

ANNULAR: *arranged in or forming a ring*

BIENNIAL: *a plant that finishes its life cycle in two growing seasons*

BISEXUAL: *containing both stamens and pistils*

BLADE: *a mass of thickened, scalelike leaves that store food*

BLOSSOM: *the flower of a plant*

BRACT: *a small, modified leaf near the base of a flower head or cluster*

CALYX: *the collective term for the sepals of a flower*

COROLLA: *the petals of a flower spoken of collectively*

CORM: *a thickened underground stem*

FAMILY: *a group of related plants*

FASCICLE: *a cluster*

FILAMENT: *the stalk of a stamen*

FLORET: *a small flower that is part of a cluster*

FROND: *the pinnate leaf of a fern; sometimes used for palm foliage as well*

GENUS: *the smallest natural group containing related but distinct species*

HERBACEOUS: *having little or no woody structure; describes plant that dies down to rootstock at end of growing season*

INFLORESCENCE: *a cluster of flowers on a single stalk*

NODE: *the place on the stem where leaves or branches originate*

OVARY: *the part of the pistil that contains the ovules*

OVULE: *immature seed*

PANICLE: *loose, diversely branching flower cluster*

PEDICLE: *the stalk of a flower*

PEDUNCLE: *the stalk of an inflorescence*

PERENNIAL: *a flower that lives for three or more growing seasons and usually flowers annually*

PERIANTH: *all the sepals and petals of a flower*

PETAL: *one of the divisions of a blossom*

PETIOLE: *the stalk of a leaf*

PISTIL: *the ovule-producing part of the male cells growing in the anther of a flower*

POLLEN: *the male cells growing in the anther of a flower.*

RACEME: *a cluster of flowers on an elongated stem*

RECEPTACLE: *the part of the flower to which the sepals, petals, stamens, and pistils are usually attached*

RHIZOME: *an underground, usually horizontal stem*

SEPAL: *a leaf of the calyx; one of the outer whorl of nonfertile parts surrounding the fertile organs of a flower*

SPATHE: *a large bract enclosing a cluster of flowers*

SPECIES: *the basic unit of classification of plants*

SPUR: *a hollow projection at the back of a flower petal*

STAMEN: *the pollen-producing organ of the flower*

STIGMA: *the bottom part of the pistil*

STIPULE: *the appendage at the base of a leaf*

STYLE: *the part of the pistil between the ovary and the stigma*

SUCCULENT: *a plant with fleshy leaves that store water*

TUBER: *thickened portion of usually underground stem in which food is stored and from which the plant grows*

UMBEL: *a flower cluster in the shape of an umbrella*

UNISEXUAL: *containing either stamens or pistils, but not both*

WHORL: *the arrangement of three or more structures at a point on the stem*

WOODY: *hard stems that retain their shape long after death*

*Thus plants and flowers of the com-
monest kind can form a pleasing diary,
because nothing which calls back to us
the remembrance of a happy moment
can be insignificant.*

GOETHE

*The simple flowers of our spring are
what I want to see again.*

JOHN KEATS

I am still devoted to the garden. But though an old man, I am but a young gardener.

THOMAS JEFFERSON

Beware: Like gardening, pressing can become the entire day.

LOKO

I owe having become a painter to flowers.

CLAUDE MONET

One of the most attractive things about the flowers is their beautiful reserve.

HENRY DAVID THOREAU

In the second month
the peach tree blooms,
but not until the ninth
the chrysanthemums: so each
must wait until his own time comes.

ANCIENT CHINESE PROVERB

Rose red and violets blue,
And all the sweetest flowers,
that in the forest grew.

EDMUND SPENSER

A flowerless room is a soul-less room to my way of thinking, but even one solitary little vase of a living flower may redeem it.

VITA SACKVILLE-WEST

I never travel without my diary. One should always have something sensational to read on the train.

OSCAR WILDE

Poetry is not an orchid, but a crocus.
Simplicity is the essence of poetry.

MAY SARTON

I like my flowers small and delicate—the taste of all gardeners, as their discrimination increases, dwindles toward the microscopic.

VITA SACKVILLE-WEST

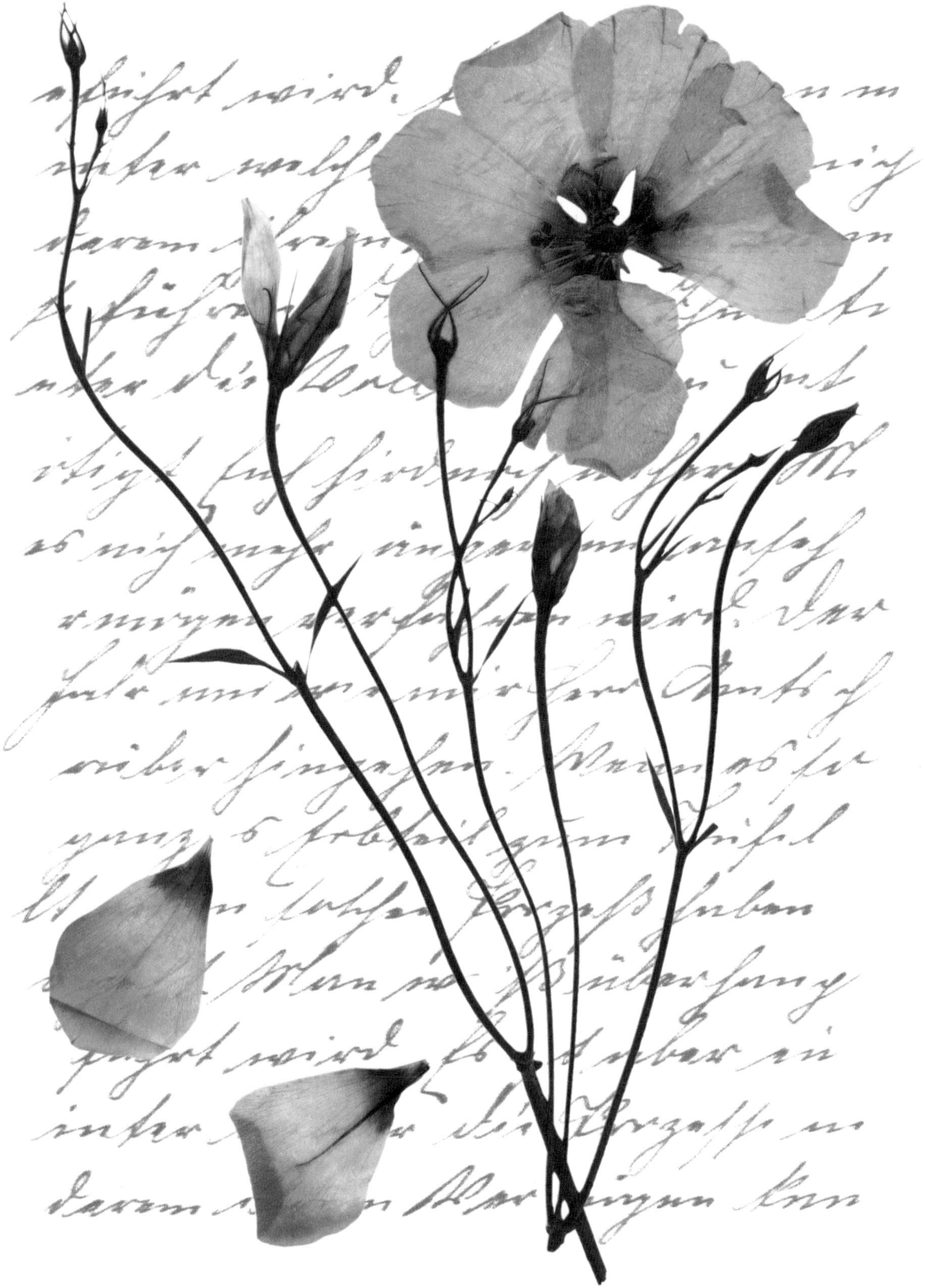

Like most cats he is devoted to the pretty catmint. It is in several places in the garden. He knows where every plant is and never passes one when we are walking together without stopping to nuzzle and nibble it . . . when he has had his first taste he will push himself right down into the middle of the plant and sometimes lie down and roll in it to get all he can of the sweet smell.

GERTRUDE JEKYLL

'Tis but a little faded flower,
But oh, how fondly dear!
Twill bring me back one golden hour,
Through many a weary year.

ELLEN C. HOWARTH

23. März 1913.

Herr Romund Dieft 15

Ich bin genötigt Euch hierdurch diefer Mittheil

...